More Fun
with Dick and Jane

Text and Illustrations by

MARC GREGORY GALLANT

NEW CONTEMPORARY READING SERIES

PENGUIN BOOKS

PENGUIN BOOKS
Viking Penguin Inc., 40 West 23rd Street,
New York, New York 10010, U.S.A.
Penguin Books Ltd, 27 Wrights Lane, London W8 5TZ
(Publishing & Editorial), and Harmondsworth,
Middlesex, England (Distribution & Warehouse)
Penguin Books Australia Ltd, Ringwood,
Victoria, Australia
Penguin Books Canada Limited, 2801 John Street,
Markham, Ontario, Canada L3R 1B4
Penguin Books (N.Z.) Ltd, 182–190 Wairau Road,
Auckland 10, New Zealand

First published in Penguin Books 1986
Published simultaneously in Canada
Reprinted 1986 (five times), 1987

Copyright © Marc Gallant, 1986
All rights reserved

Library of Congress Cataloging in Publication Data
Gallant, Marc, 1946–
More fun with Dick and Jane.
(New contemporary reading series)
1. Readers (Primary)—Anecdotes, facetiae, satire,
etc. I. Title. II. Series.
PN6231.R36G35 1986   818'.5402   85-25990
ISBN 0 14 00.7692 1

Printed in the United States of America by
R. R. Donnelley & Sons Company, Crawfordsville, Indiana
Set in Century Expanded

TO THE READER

More Fun with Dick and Jane is an all-new primer written for the millions of people who readily recall that immortal line: "See Spot Run." In this new book the principal characters Dick, Jane and Sally have grown up.

Dick, now almost forty, is a systems engineer for a public utility. Married to Susan, a minor character from the original series, Dick is a quiet, well-meaning father to three boys — Brad, Rick and Adam. Dick works tirelessly, pays his bills promptly and has a fascination for gadgets; he is also an avid golfer with a secret ambition to get a hole in one.

Jane is a thirty-eight-year-old divorcée. She lives with her two daughters Robin and Jessica, in an impeccably clean house in a suburb of Dayton, Ohio (about a half hour drive from her brother Dick). By day Jane works as a loan officer in a downtown bank; after hours she brings incredible zeal to her job as a direct distributor for Amway. Jane is focused, serious and very independent.

Sally, also known as "baby" in the pre-primers, is now thirty-six. She has been married and divorced twice but unlike her sister she does not seem noticeably affected by either marriage. Sally is a Public Relations Director for a large winery. She lives and works in Mill Valley, California, traveling to the winery in nearby Napa every other week. Although she is fond of her nephews and nieces, Sally has little to do with her family. She did however return to Ohio for Zeke's funeral (Zeke was the seldom-seen caretaker who was forever raking up leaves).

Both grandparents passed away some time ago; Father died somewhat prematurely in 1981. Mother now in her seventies lives in a retirement home about a half day's drive from Dayton. She enjoys bowling and has recently returned from an organized tour of the Holy Land. *Puff*, the family cat died years ago and is rarely mentioned. *Spot?* Well . . . read on.

STORIES

Some New Faces

More Family Fun

Life with Jane

A Visit with Sally

Some New Faces

Dick

Jane

Sally

Susan

Rick, Adam and Brad

Jessica and Robin

Grandmother

Spot

Agatha-May

More Family Fun

See It Go Up

"Look, look!" said Brad.

"Look at my stunt kite.

See it go up.

Up, up, up."

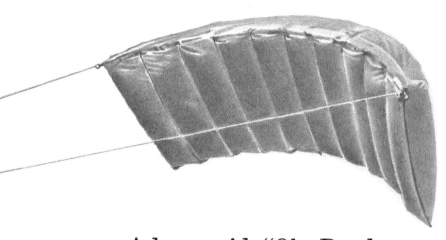

Adam said, "Oh, Brad.
Your stunt kite is rad.
Totally rad!"

"Oh, yes!" said Rick.
"It is rad."

Brad said, "Oh, look!
Look at my stunt kite.
It is coming down.
It is coming down fast.
Hurry! We must find it."

"Oh, oh, oh!" said Brad.

"Look at Father.

He is wearing my stunt kite."

"Oh, Brad!" said Adam.

"Father is grossed out."

Something for Adam

"Oh, Dad!" whispered Brad.

"It will soon be Adam's birthday.

Can you guess what Adam wants?

He would like a dog.

Can we get a dog for Adam?

Can we please?"

"We will see," said Dick.

"We will see."

It was soon Adam's birthday.

"Happy Birthday!" said Dick.

"Happy Birthday!" said Susan.

"We have something for you.

We have something you will like."

"Oh, boy!" said Adam.

"I can hardly wait."

"Oh, wow!" cried Adam.
"You have bought me a dog —
a little black and white dog.
It is perfect!
It is exactly what I wanted.
Oh, thank you!" said Adam.
"Thank you for the dog."

Adam said, "What will I call him?
What would be a good name?"
"I know!" said Dick.
"You can call him Spot."
"Yes, yes!" said Adam.
"I can call him Spot."
"Bow-wow!" barked Spot.
"Bow-wow! Bow-wow!"

A Walk with Spot

Dick said, "Come, Adam.

We will walk with Spot."

"Yip-ee!" cried Adam.

"But, Father!

Why do you have a shovel?"

"Oh, Adam," laughed Dick.

"This is not a shovel.

This is a pooper-scooper."

"A pooper-scooper," said Adam.

"Yuck! Yuck!"

A Big Big Surprise

"It is Saturday," said Dick.

"We could drive by the farm."

"Oh, yes!" said Susan.

"We have not seen the farm

in such a long time.

Let us hurry!

Let us hurry to the farm."

"Hurray!" said Brad.

"We can go in the K-car."

"Hurray!" said Adam.

"Hurray!" said Rick.

"It is fun to ride in the K-car.

It is fun to go to the farm.

Let us hurry!"

"We will soon be there," said Dick.

"We will soon be at the farm."

"Yip-ee!" said Brad.

"Yip-ee!" said Adam.

"Yip-ee!" said Rick.

"It does not take long," said Susan.

"It does not take long in a K-car."

"Oh, dear!" said Dick.

"This is not the farm.

The farm has been destroyed."

"Dear, me!" said Susan.

"The Clarks must have sold it.

Well, never mind.

We will have some lunch."

"Yip-ee!" yelled the boys.

"Yip-ee!"

Good News

"Oh, Dad!" cried Brad.

"Ms. Stanley says my Language
Arts paper is excellent.

I might even win a trip."

"Go for it!" said Dick. "Go for it!"

"Oh, really Dad," said Brad.

"No one says – go for it – anymore."

"Oh, sorry!" blushed Dick.

Cookie Chain

Susan said, "Here, boys.

Here are some cookies."

"Oh, Mother!" said Brad.

"These cookies are awesome."

"And how!" said Rick.

"You should start a cookie chain."

"Oh, Rick!" blushed Susan.

"My own cookie chain?"

A Good Guess

Dick said, "Look, boys,
I have a package.
Do you know what it is?"
"I know!" said Rick and Adam.
"I know!" said Brad.
"It is an Apple Macintosh
with 128K RAM."

"You have guessed," said Dick.

It is a Macintosh for my family."

"Oh, dear!" said Susan.

"128K RAM!

I will never understand it."

"Relax, Mother!" said Brad.

"The Macintosh is user-friendly."

"Oh!" said Susan.

Dick Has a Headache

"I have a headache," said Dick,
and it's got tension
written all over it."
"Here, Dick!" said Susan.
"Take this tablet.
It has five grains of painkiller."
"Five grains!" said Dick.
"Yes!" said Susan.
"And it's coated too."

Fair Trade

"Oh, Adam!" said Jessica.

"You have GI-Joe.*

Please, may I play with him?"

"OK!" said Adam.

"You can play with my GI-Joe.

I will play with your Barbie."**

"Woop-ee!" cried Jessica.

"Woop-ee!"

More Fun with Toys

"Ra-ta-ta-tat!" yelled Brad.

"You're dead — D-E-A-D "

"Ka-boom!" cried Rick.

"You're wasted, Adam."

"No way!" said Adam.

"I am Mr. T. and I say
you're both dead — D-E-A-D "

Jane Remembers

"Surprise, surprise!" said Jane.

"I have brought you a drink."

"Oh, Jane!" said Dick.

"Is that what I think it is?"

"Yes, Dick," laughed Jane.

"It's your favorite drink —
it's red Kool-Aid."

41

Adam's Wish

Adam said, "Oh, Mother!
I miss Grandmother.
Can we visit her?"
"Yes, Adam," said Susan.
"We will visit her soon."
"Yeah sure," said Adam.
"That's what you said last month."

Life with Jane

A Special Book

Jessica said, "Look, Mother.

Here is a letter.

Here is a big big letter."

"Oh, Jessica!" laughed Jane.

"This is not a letter.

This is a catalogue.

This is a catalogue from L. L. Bean."

"What is a catalogue?" said Jessica,
"Can you tell me?"
"Yes, Jessica," said Jane,
"I can tell you.
A catalogue is a special book,
a book with pictures of things to buy."
"Oh, boy!" said Jessica,
"I like catalogues!"

Can You Guess?

Jessica said, "Can you guess?

Can you guess who it is?"

"Yes!" said Jane.

"I can guess.

It is Jessica.

It is my baby Jessica."

"Oh, Jessica!" cried Jane.

"What have you done to your hair?
You are a punker!"

"Relax!" said Jessica.

"It is only make-believe.

I am not a real punker.

I am your baby Jessica."

A Lesson for Robin

Jane said, "Look, Robin, look.
It is easy to make a quiche.
Just pour and bake."
"Oh, yes!" said Robin
"It is easy, Mother.
And we can microwave it!"

Product Day

"Here, Mother," said Robin.

"Here is your Amway.*

It is very, very heavy."

"Oh, Robin," said Jane.

"Today is product day.

I must work hard.

"If I work really hard . . .

*A trademark of Amway Corporation.

I could become a double diamond."

"Double diamond?" asked Robin.

"What is a double diamond?"

"Well," said Jane.

"Let's just say a double diamond
makes lots and lots of money."

"Could I be a double diamond?"

"Yes, Robin," said Jane.

"If you work hard you can have it all."

A Visit with Sally

Keeping Fit

"Look, look!" said Sally.
"Can you do what I do?
Legs over . . . and stretch.
Relax, one, two.
One, two and stretch.
Can you do what I do?"

Jessica said, "Look, Aunt Sally.
I can do what you do.
Left leg out . . . and stretch.
Relax, one, two.
One, two and stretch.
I can go for the burn."
"Oh, Jessica," laughed Sally
"You can do what I do."

Light Days

Robin said, "Look, look!
Look at Aunt Sally.
She is falling down.

Down, down, down."

"Oh, Robin!" said Jessica.
"Aunt Sally is falling down.
She is falling fast.

Fast, fast, fast."

Good Clean Fun

Sally said, "Oh, girls!
Isn't this fun?
Isn't it fun to be creative?"
"Yes, yes!" said Jessica.
"It is fun, Aunt Sally.
But what will we draw?
Will we draw a house?"

"Oh, no!" said Sally.

"It is boring to draw a house.

We will do an abstract."

"An abstract?" said Robin.

"Do we have abstracts in Ohio?"

"Of course you do," laughed Sally.

"Of course you do,"

Neat Stuff

"Esprit!"* said Robin.

"Oh, Aunt Sally.

You wear the neatest stuff."

"Thank you," said Sally.

"I do like to project a

Sharper Image!"**

*Esprit is the Registered Trademark of a San Francisco based clothing manufacturer.
**Sharper Image is the Registered Trademark of a San Francisco based mail-order house.

An Evening with Sally

"Oh, Craig!" said Sally.

"You are just in time for dinner."

"Terrific!" said Craig.

"Look, Sally! It is for you.

It is a flowering cactus."

"Oh, Craig!" blushed Sally.

"For me."

"Oh, Sally!" said Craig.
"Wild Mushroom Salad with
Radicchio and Radish Sprouts!
It's my favorite!"
"And that's not all!" said Sally.
"Later we will have Cold Poached
Chicken with Walnut Basil Pesto."
"Oh, Sally!" cried Craig.
"You are such a gourmet."

The Party

"Oh, phooey!" said Sally.

"I am out of business cards.

And I must have cards for my party.

What will I do?"

"Oh, Aunt Sally," said Robin.

"No business cards!

What will you do?"

"Hurry girls," said Sally.
"We must hurry.
We must go to Quick-Print."

"Hurry, hurry, hurry," said Jessica.
"Mother is right, Aunt Sally.
You are on the fast track."
"Oh, Jessica," blushed Robin.

"Well now," said Sally.
"Let me see . . .
  Who can I invite?
There's Craig and Jason and . . .
of course — some business friends."
"Business friends?" asked Robin.
"Sure!" said Sally. "You know —
people I can network with."

Sally said, "Come girls.

Come meet my wonderful friends.

This is Winston, my broker . . .

Hisako, my new friend from EST* . .

and Daryl, my accountant."

*Erhard Seminars Training is a California-based human potential group which gained popularity during the seventies.

"Oh, Aunt Sally," said Robin.

"You have wonderful friends."

"Oh, yes!" said Jessica.

"And it's fun to party Aunt Sally —
but can we network now?"

TO THE READER

More Fun with Dick and Jane is the first primer of the NEW CONTEMPORARY READING SERIES. It follows, after a considerable lapse in time, a number of basic pre-primers and primers which you will undoubtedly remember.

This new primer, like all previous ones, develops a totally new vocabulary. It also contains words which appear in their colloquial or casual form. This is the first time such informal words have been included in a primer. A good example is "rad" on page twenty-one: *"Oh, Brad. Your stunt kite is rad."* *"Rad"* is a popular form of the word *radical* which in this case means: *great; terrific; super* or *really neat.*

Readers will also discover words which cannot be found in any ordinary dictionary. Examples include: *Yuck; Yip-ee; pooper-scooper; K-car; RAM; user-friendly; GI-Joe; Barbie; Woop-ee; Ra-ta-ta-tat; Ka-boom* and *Mr. T.* While readers are not openly encouraged to use these words frequently it should be recognized that they have become legitimized through common use.

VOCABULARY LIST

The following list contains 242 words not used in any previous program.

MORE FAMILY FUN

20	Brad	23	wearing	26	wow		barked
	stunt		grossed		cried	28	walk
	kite		out		bought		Yip-ee
21	Adam	24	Dad		perfect		why
	your		whispered		exactly		shovel
	rad		be	27	call	29	pooper-
	totally		would		him		scooper
	Rick		like		be		Yuck
22	coming	25	hardly		name	30	Saturday
	Hurry		wait		know		could

drive
by
seen
such
long
time
Let
us
31 Hurray
K-car
32 take
33 has
been
destroyed
Clarks
sold
never
mind
some
lunch
yelled
boys
34 Ms. Stanley
says
Language

Arts
paper
excellent
might
even
win
trip
really
says
anymore
blushed
Sorry
35 chain
some
These
awesome
how
should
start
own
36 package
Apple
MacIntosh
128K
RAM

37 guessed
understand
Relax
user-friendly
38 Has
Headache
it's
got
tension
written
over
Take
tablet
five
grains
of
painkiller
coated
39 Jessica
GI-Joe
him
OK
Barbie
Whoop-ee
40 More

Ra-ta-ta-tat
You're
dead
Kaboom
wasted
way
Mr. T.
both
41 Remembers
brought
drink
favorite
Kool-Aid
42 Wish
miss
visit
soon
that's
last
month

LIFE WITH JANE

44 letter
catalogue
L. L. Bean
45 tell
special
book
pictures
things
buy
like
46 —
47 only
believe
real
48 Lesson
Robin
easy
quiche
Just
pour
bake
microwave
49 Product
Day
Amway
heavy
Today
must
work
hard
really
50 become
double
diamond
lots
money
A VISIT WITH SALLY

52 Keeping
Fit
Legs
stretch
53 Aunt
Left
burn
54 Light
Days
falling
55 —
56 Clean
girls
Isn't
creative
draw
57 boring
an
abstract
Ohio
course
58 Neat
Stuff
Esprit
wear
neatest
project
Sharper
Image
59 Evening
Craig
time
dinner
Terrific
flowering
cactus
60 Wild
Mushroom

Salad
Radicchio
Radish
Sprouts
favorite
that's
Later
Cold
Poached
Chicken
Walnut
Basil
Pesto
such
gourmet
61 Party
phooey
business
cards
62 Quick-Print
right
track
63 invite
There's
Jason
Sure
people
network
64 wonderful
Winston
broker
Hisako
EST
Daryl
accountant
65 —

ACKNOWLEDGMENTS

I would like to thank the many people who helped me in the preparation of this book. I am indebted to Morton Mint, president of Penguin Canada for making a commitment to the project while it was still 'just an outline.' A special thank you is due Gerry Howard my editor at Penguin New York for his unbridled enthusiasm and for his incredible patience.

To prepare new *Dick and Jane* illustrations it was necessary to first select models and produce photographic reference material. A number of people were especially helpful in this regard. Firstly, there is my friend David Coffin. Without his good-natured support and sense of humor I might well have let the winter skies turn in on me. Equally helpful was Alexis Magaro. She not only led me to Sally; she graciously provided transportation to many of the photo sessions.

I also want to thank Patrick Harris (Dick) for his generous assistance and Charles Schmalz for his good advice.

A large debt of gratitude is owed to many others who gave both time and energy to this project. They include: David Baxendale; Joshua Brough *(Rick)*; Zachary Brough *(Brad)*; Shelby Brough *(Susan)*; Sarah Butler; Tristan Butler *(Adam)*; Jon Carrol; Marilyn Crenshaw *(Sally)*; Nancy and Douglas Davis; Ronald Davis; Nicholas Dawe; Beatrice Doiron; Regis Duffy; Joe Freedman; Peggy Frost; Phyllis Gallant; Ted Gamauf; Berl Garrett; Dan Hart; Suzanne Hauss; Michael Jardine; Dorena Kelly; Robyn Langhorst; Steve LeBoeuf; John Lewis; Judy Loeser; Bea Losito; Charles Lovett; Keith McKeen; Brady Meyring; Bob Minardi; Drew Neeb; Jean-Claude Rivalland; Marika Roblin *(Jessica)*; Samara Roblin *(Robin)*; Will Roblin; Ira Rudikoff; Judy Sato; Dr. Ray Shapiro; Emily Shaw; Rosemary Silva; Thatcher *(Spot)*; David Vandergriff; Bonnie Walker *(Jane)*; Pamela Walker.

PENGUIN BOOKS

More Fun with Dick and Jane

Marc Gallant began his formal education with the *Dick and Jane* pre-primers and has never quite recovered. Born in 1946 in Prince Edward Island, Canada, he has worked as a photographer and as a graphic designer. He is also an enthusiastic traveler, enjoys flying kites and has a keen interest in cooking. (A good part of the advance for this book was spent on tin-lined copper saucepans.) Mr. Gallant is also author of *The Cow Book*.